TRUMP 2020

TRUMP 2020

Dr. Randy White

To order additional copies of this book, contact:
Xlibris
1-888-795-4274
www.Xlibris.com
Orders@Xlibris.com
802745

Contents

Foreword

Dr. White highlights the fact that America is at a tipping point in history. Foreign and globalist powers have corrupted the democratic governance of the United States to such an extent that American citizens no longer have much control over their own country. In **Trump 2020**, we see what the deterioriation of values has done to America and why the nation needs to change its political direction to avoid economic domination by outside forces. Learn where we need to go from here. *"For lack of guidance, a nation falls"* *Proverbs 11:14*

Ken Schultz
Retired Insurance Agent and Farmer

In his precient work, Trump 2020, Dr. White paints a vivid depiction of the United States and the current obstacles that we face as a nation that must be addressed in order to continue to thrive as a nation. One nation after another is standing in line attempting, in an abundance of ways, to take advantage of the fractured landscape that presently divides the country. Line by line Dr. White lays out the issues we face with precision and skill. A house divided can not stand and Trump 2020 shows us a more perfect path to not only avoid a dismal fate, but to, as a nation thrive on the world stage brighter than ever before.

Forrest Jones
Financial Advisor

Dr. Randy White has been in accounting business for over 40 years, yet he is not your typical accountant. He has been and still is a conscientious observer of the trends in society. It is through this lens that he has observed the current state of affairs in the United States.

Dr. White is a husband, father, grandfather, foster parent, faithful member of his church and successful businessman. He has a lot of insight into the human condition.

In this book he identifies the Silent Majority and sheds light on just who represents this segment in society. He compares the current office of the Presidency with historical ones. He gets to the source of the truth behind student loans and the real motive for making billions of dollars available to college students.

In this book he covers important topics such as the economy, immigration, the media, foreign trade with China, the national debt and education.

At the very least the reader will come away with balance and perspective on the world today.

Scott Baker
Chasewood Bank
Vice President - Commercial Lending

Prologue

As a silent majority member, I have watched the political scene over the past several years, finding that the Washington DC spectrum is un-American. The political division is now at the point of no return, with the issues of ethics, religious and morality falling to levels not previously seen in America.

Our elected officials are not creating or defining legislation for the betterment of the public, but the politicians are more in line with each of their respective political parties. The legislation process does not involve what is good for the public, but what is good for the party.

The state of the finances of our federal government is in a point of disarray as seen with the government's debt, which has climbed to levels never seen in the history of our country. We as a country continue to give billions of dollars to countries who despise Americans. As a country, we have never learned the lesson that you can't buy loyalty. In addition, we ruin countries by taking out their incentives to learn and grow. Look at the Native American Indian; look at American Samoa during WWII. In fact, look at the current family unit with kids in their 40's still living with their parents, and grandparents whom are raising their grandkids, unheard of in the history of America.

Ethics, morals, human freedom, drugs, credit, social media, entitlements, government is not the answer; all these areas have changed from the 1950's which, in my opinion, were the best days for the American family. Today, men want to be women, women want to be men, and another group now is not sure which gender they are or want to be. As the late and great Reggie White said, "Homosexuality is a decision, it's not a race".

Our forefathers were men of great integrity and were visionaries. America was created as one nation under God as a Christian nation with the right to religious freedoms. America has turned from these early fundamentals of our democracy. Today Americans on the Sabbath are at home, foregoing the church with their respective recreational endeavors. On September 1, 2001, America was rudely awakened by a barbaric attack on our sovereign soil with over 3,000 citizens perishing within an hour of one another. This terroristic act offered a change in our day-to-day lives. Churches were filled to capacity with people seeking answers from their pastors or priest. Where does America stand in the end times? How does America fare in biblical prophecy? These were but a few of the questions the non-religious sector of America was asking. Over a short period of time, however, these individuals whom flocked to the church for answers went back to their weekly traditions of sleeping in on Sunday or other recreational practices.

This book does not offer an accounting of day-to-day activities of many officials in the public's eye as the writer has no personal relationship with any politician or political figure in the media today. Instead, this book represents the lifetime observation of an average American who has gotten up and worked every day, attends the church of his choice and the father of 17 children raised (10 of those as a non-paid foster parent) and presently a grandfather of 15.

Historically our government is controlled by two political parties which has developed to a method which I refer to as running with the pack. When an elected official goes to Congress they are voted in by their constituents based upon the candidates' political platform. Each newly elected official has visions of changing the world and many have good ideas for their constituents as well as all Americans. But this is where the buck stops; the elected officials have found the Washington DC culture to be that of what the agenda for each party in DC. As I have said all along, an elected official is "either the problem or the solution." The politician makes a decision early on in their political career to either change their political agenda to that of the party they are affiliated with or go independent to that of the political party.

When this process happens, the politician moves away from his or her election platform to that of what the party wants, thus there is no representation in DC. Being a Democrat or a Republican should not be the issue, but the newly elected politician should legislate law for the good of the whole and not for a select group.

There is nothing special about this writer as we attempt to compile 50-years of observations of our political process. This book will be reflective of the major topics affecting all Americans in 2020.

1. State of Affairs - Washington, DC

The state of affairs in our nation's capital over the past 60 years has been a mess from all aspects, including historical organizations and agreements, the federal deficit, foreign trade imbalance, numerous international agreements from NATO to the Paris Accord, the SALT Agreement; and on and on. Washington DC is now reflective of representatives in positions of power whom are not part of the solution to our nation's problems, but are imbedded in office with each representing a political party strategy and not the views of their constituents.

Both houses of Congress can never agree on any issue, as the House and Senate always vote along party lines. This type of government is directed to our Congressmen and Senators whom seek money and power. This same self-seeking type of ideology has ruined our judicial system of government. Years ago my late father, a medic and bronze star recipient in WWII, told me that many a newly elected Congressman or Senator were good men/women when elected, yet years later these trusted officials quickly learned that if they want to get their legislation passed, they had to run with their political party or end up being the lone wolf.

A classic example of this is Senator Ron Paul out of Lake Jackson, Texas, a small-town south of Houston carved out of the swamp in the 1940's by the Dow Chemical Company. In his decades in office, Dr. Ron Paul never passed one piece of legislation which supported his senatorial district during his tenure in office. Dr. Paul has originated numerous legislative proposals which never passed due to not being accepted by his own party. One will remember, Dr. Paul advocated the gold standard, as our Congress took us off the gold standard 40-years ago. Now the Department of Treasury just prints money when needed. Dr. Paul was correct with his assessment of the gold standard, but America is in a free fall with increased debt backed by that of a sovereign government. This fiscal process needs to stop.

The average person in America does not understand that many of the decisions made in Congress have a direct bearing on each person as well as numerous generations to come.

The era of never paying down the debt of the United States of America is and has been a concern of many ever since President Lyndon Baines Johnson borrowed $47 billion in 1968 from the Social Security Trust and Medicare Trust Funds and moved over to the general budget as a fix to balance the federal budget for that particular year. "A Presidential commission composed of distinguished congressional fiscal leaders and other prominent Americans recommended this year that we adopt a new budget approach. I am carrying out their recommendations in this year's budget. This budget, therefore, for the first time accurately covers all Federal expenditures and all Federal receipts, including for the first time in one budget $47 billion from the social security, Medicare, highway, and other trust funds." (Smith, 2014)

Over the past 40 years Congress and the office of the President of the United States has continually robbed from the American people's trust fund. Today the trust fund only has IOU's in lieu of billions of dollars of accumulated cash build up. If one were to invest $47 billion at 2% over the past 52 years, that accumulation of money would be enough money to completely wipe out the national debt of over $22 trillion and have a surplus of $109 trillion.

According to the Congressional Research Service Report," the Social Security Trust Fund is solvent until the year 2034" (Huston, 2019). From a balance sheet perspective, the Social Security Trust Fund appears solvent, but in reality the trust fund has IOU's commonly known as "Special Obligation Bonds" or a single purpose bond issue. "The brutal truth is this $2.85 trillion fund, has no money". (Adler, 2017) Our government produces these financial reports which are very misleading and if the Trust Fund were to do immediate cash call, our federal government would be in default. Not a real comforting fact.

Every four to eight years when a new administration enters Washington DC, grand ideas are divided by party lines. Typically, whichever party is in power, they eventually leave office with the same result, a divided America and an increased cash deficit with no end in sight. Presently with the emergence of the Trump administration we are seeing the Office of the President attempting to combat real issues from the perspective of a non-politician. We are now seeing the opposing party in a defensive mode while foregoing governance and working daily to find any type of substance of impropriety from the Office of the President.

As a senior citizen and a common man, I have never seen a party so out for vengeance with their leadership team running out of control. The country had sixteen years of the Clinton and the Obama administration which all governance continued as the normal course of business from day-to-day. The surprise vote of the Electoral College in which the Trump administration won office by a slim margin, but an election result that overturned almost every pollster with their election experts, raised the question of "Why did this happen?". The results of the election were simple, the silent majority spoke and they were heard.

America used to be great, our greatest generation fought and died for our right to maintain democracy attributed to being born American. Freedom of speech, freedom of religion and the right to capitalism are but some of our freedoms that many in this new generation fail to realize, as they are so removed from this prior time of the day infamy. With Pearl Harbor, all Americans, no matter what race, nationally, or religion, bound together to meet a very evil force from Germany. During this time period, America was at risk, millions of men/women gave their lives to ensure our laws and values continue for perpetuity.

When viewing the world, America is the only major country in the world which offers individual freedom, opportunity for advancement and a rule of law to protect each and every citizen. There is now a flood of immigrants entering the United States to seek a better way of life for their immediate family as well as their grandkids and future generations to come. No other country offers the resources and opportunities for advancement.

2. Current History of the Office of the President of the United States

The office of the President of the United States represents the most powerful office in the world. The historical significance of the office is well documented and the record of each President is archived as no other country in the world. This rich history is what makes America.

Presidents come and go, as well as do the political parties they represent. The 1950's, as previously mentioned, represented a healing in America after the Great War. The 1960's represented change in the social, economic, education and the face of the workforce.

But also during this time of the 1960's social unrest began to unravel. That era brought an increase in drugs, sexual promiscuity, inflation and simply keeping up with the Jones.

The social and economic face of America changed. Previously after the war, you could just about gauge the economic level of a family by where they lived, the vehicle they drove and the school their children went to. In today's world with the advent of computers and software, the social image is more important to a person, as compared to their actual level of economic standing. Finance and credit cards have allowed a person to show visible prosperity while behind the curtain, another story of high credit card debt, no positive cash flow; but the outward appearance of living the American dream. Somewhat like our federal government with our level of debt.

Almost every President of the United States has held a law degree, and most have become great orators in being able to deliver their position to the general public. The average American will never run for office, as only the most powerful people with great financial support will move through the masses to arrive on a party ticket.

The Obama as well as the Trump administrations represent the silent majority whom want change in our nation's Capital. This one underlying truth is why each party was elected, as neither President was well known within the political arena. The silent majority wants change in the way our government is being ran and the general public opted to elect officials whom promised change.

Our country is different; we have the rule of law by each state and governance by each. The federal government only comes into play when disputes arise between states, as outlined by our forefathers. Our rule of law is what often separates our country from other major countries such as Russia and China whom have a Communistic form of government.

The Office of President of the United States represents the executive division of government as there are checks and balances within America. The judicial branch represents the law making division of our government as the judicial branch is divided into the House of Representatives or the United States Senate. Before law is passed, both houses must pass legislation in the same language and the agreed to law is then forwarded to the Office of the President for his signature to complete the judicial process. This checks and balance system of government often separates our government from other governments such as seen in China or Russia and other socially dependent countries such as Venezuela.

3. The Silent Majority

Since the Reagan years, our House and Senate seemed to come together with bi-partisan support for the good of the law. Since this time period we have had both parties in office.

After the tenure of George Bush Sr., America saw a shift in the divisions between the two parties which changed almost overnight, as the silent majority again spoke. The economy was the key factor as Bush Sr. was elected to only one term. This change ushered in President Bill Clinton, who was elected as a little-known Governor out of Arkansas; this began a two-term Democratic Party rule.

The Clinton administration ushered in a period of Congressional investigations, due to close friends of the Clinton family mysteriously dying and sexual misconduct by the highest-ranking political official in our government. So much for the social morals in our nation. With America in constant turmoil the voters turned back the watch to the Democratic Party with the Obama years.

President Obama won an unprecedented term which had many a political expert puzzled. The Obama victory was nothing more than an outpouring of protest and pent up hostility toward the Washington DC political process. The silent majority turns out to vote and their votes can be described as unison support for change. The political process in DC began a deeply divided process of polarization of the two parties.

The silent majority sees what is going on in DC and they do not care for this process. Many a talented Congressman man or woman have been elected from their area of representation only to arrive in DC and upon their first day they are recruited into the pack. In order to survive DC, you must run with the pack or be ostracized. This situation is very evident when the public watches the annual Presidential "State of the Union" message. The party in power applauds often while standing and the opposing party sits stiff necked with no emotional response.

The public views this across nation in their living rooms as the issues are not really discussed.

The real issue boils down to what your political party says about the issue. In review of political parties, Senator Ron Paul of Lake Jackson never ran with the pack and over his tenure in DC never originated one piece of legislation for his constituents which passed both the house and senate. In Senator Paul's defense, important legislation was not passed during his time in DC. Dr. Paul had his own agenda during his term in the Senate, but often his legislation ran contrary to his political party or in my term, of not running with the pack.

Again, in the 2016 presidential election, the Democratic Party with their candidate Hillary Clinton had the clear lead in all the polls. The election was hers to lose and lose she did.

The silent majority came out to vote with one united concern, get this country back on top as the premier country in the world. The results showed the public wanted change, they want job opportunity, they want secure borders, and they want the government to be fiscally responsible. These are but a few of the voting points the American people mandated, and the result was contrary to what the political world has previously known, with the election of a businessman, President Donald Trump.

Many a political analyst or almost all the pollsters said no way would a non-attorney businessperson be elected to the most powerful position in the world; but it happened!

Donald Trump as an American saw what was going on in DC and collectively the silent majority of Americans went to the polls in support of change. President Trump mandated change and change was made. The expert political analysts were amazed by the immediate change from the financial markets on Wall Street.

The American public demanded change, and change came. The media from day-one was amazed at how the stock market jumped with the final election tally. Typically, the markets do not like change or even more, the unknown. The Republican Party was now back in vogue with both houses along with the White House.

The first year of the Trump administration is reflective of the Democratic Party in denial. The disbelief of our electoral process and even calling for recounts in various states proved their disbelief. The Democratic denial process has continued to evolve over the first two years of the Trump administration.

At present, the leadership of the Democratic Party has no answers to the new economic conditions seen in America. There is a feeling of hope and opportunity in America, as not seen since the Reagan administration.

4. The World Today

As a young boy growing up in America, my parents were part of the "greatest generation". The time period after WWII and into the 1950's represented a new era for our nation's veterans.

The family unit was evident all across the nation; patriotism was at a very high level. Our GI's that survived the war years came home to peace and reuniting with their families. History also tells us of the sacrifices of the American women in the workforce who came out of the home environment to go into the workforce in support of the war years. These women were the unknown heroes of WWII.

Having worked in the business world for the past 40-years has allowed me to see the world as it has evolved. Historically, Russia's economy revolves around their oil exports. Russia being a Communistic country ruled by intimidation and threats by government officials with the majority of cities in the country is controlled by family units, commonly known as the mob. These families are locally known by the locals as persons to stay away from. Even Vladimir Putin has been in office for years and somehow he has become a billionaire as a so called public servant. One only has to look at export oil with high commissions paid out to Putin with his Switzerland bank accounts; a billionaire working as a public official.

The Chinese have a long history of theft from foreign companies who have a presence in their country. If you will, go back to the USA Air Force spy plane shot down in China. With continued negotiations between the two countries, the US finally was able to retrieve the plane, but it was retrieved in parts. This one incident showed the world how technology is developed in China. I for one have seen two other situations with the Chinese in the 1980's and 1990's of Chinese personnel hired by American companies who developed software for the company, but to be caught later in selling the software out the back door.

Mexico, our neighbors to the south, offers two bordering countries have currency differences in larger portions; the natural progression of mass exodus to a capitalist society which offers individual opportunities is a progressive process. Additionally, with such a large currency difference, there is inherent tendency for graft and corruption within the governmental agencies. Thus, Mexico will always have payoffs for local officials which has gone on historically.

This process has been widely exposed with the emergence of the cartels and the drug trade.

Canada is our other border neighbor to the north, yet their currency is comparable to the US Dollar exchange; there is no history of a flow south of Canadians into the USA or corruption as seen with the Mexican officials.

The Middle East representative of the origin of the world has, for centuries, always been a source of human right issues, women's rights and the freedom of religion. Many a former President of the United States has tried to intervene with several of the Middle East countries which are all anarchies. There is little rule of law as the Muslim religion appears to run against Christianity.

Several of these countries harbor terrorists and have done so for decades. America has been looked upon as the police of the world, yet the history of American politics typically protect the foreign interest of countries which have a natural resource of hydrocarbons.

The continent of Africa is somewhat desolate with life expectancy in some areas up to 40-years. Infant death rates are very high and disease and pestilence are common causes of death.

Over the past few years Bill and Linda Gates have brought attention to these third world countries and they are using their resources to combat loss of life. We should all acknowledge and support their endeavors. Africa in general offers no real commodity as a resource, thereby little effort is given to stop the brutal killings seen within the African nations.

If you take away America, Canada and parts of Europe, the world is made up of less developed countries that offer their peoples little hope for the future. Their next generation will more than likely be similar to what their parents experienced during their lives. Again, the quality of life and life expectancies are much less than that seen today in America.

5. The Economy

With the election of a new party beginning January 2017, the Republican Party holds the Senate and the Office of the President. The House of Representatives is controlled by the Democratic Party.

With the surprising results of the 2016 election, a non-political President was elected by the general population for a four-year term. The Trump administration was voted in by the silent majority and this silent majority wants change. Washington, DC is populated by the politically elite, while the general population consists of hard-working people residing in an urban setting with very high cost of living. Not much room for advancement for a minority without education or a family history of prosperity. Our urban areas represent challenge for education, healthcare, and opportunity. The rural areas are not faced with such drastic problems, but their issues are seen in other forms.

The 2016 election results brought about several immediate changes within the stock markets, as our stock markets never like change or the unknown. When the Trump administration was ushered in, the stock market took off. Again, pent up demand and the silent majority wanting change. The first order of business for the Trump administration was to cut the tax rates for both individuals as well as the corporate tax rate. The top tax rate of individuals was lowered from 39.6% to 37% and the Corporation rate was reduced by 40% from 35% to a fixed 21%. Never before in the history of our federal tax tables have tax rates been reduced in a material amount.

These tax rates spurred corporate hiring which assisted in driving the GNP and promoted economic growth. America began to prosper after turmoil's time of the recession which began in 2008 and ran through 2013. From a technical issue, the recession ran only two years, but in practical sense, the recession was reflective of slow growth over the next three years. This specific recession was one of the longest recessions in the history of America. With the reduction of the corporate tax rate, companies were able to hire personnel and this one event helped lower the national unemployment rate to levels never before seen. The unemployment levels were across the board with all races of the workforce contributing to low unemployment lines with all of States.

6. Student Loans

Our government has made college accessible to all who want to attend. Student loans are available and are automatic when applying at an accredited institution of higher education. Students who choose to attend a trade school or college or university are in effect making a choice to upgrade their skills in an effort to obtain the American dream in obtaining a better position in life. The trade schools and universities offer this medium of exchange for improvement. Companies often require higher education as the company views this as an entry level into their specific business.

The student loan system is currently in crises. Approximately 78,000 students are making no attempt to repay their loan from the government. Over one-trillion dollars of loans are not even in forbearance, but just in arrears. There is no reason for this, each student whom is in default has been educated and trained for advancement within our democracy and capitalistic system of economy.

The Department of Education should work with the IRS in identifying who these 78,000 people are and go after each, similar to a credit collection company. The majorities of these 78,000 former students are working and file taxes. The Social Security Administration has active records of where they are working, and the Department of Education should contact each of their employers and withhold a fixed amount or allow each former student in arrears to agree on an amount to be paid back over time.

7. Immigration

When President George W. Bush was in office, he attempted to originate the foreign worker program designed to allow foreign workers to enter the country with a 6-month to one-year work visa directed toward farm works, service works and other non-technical positions. The public turned this down. Since that time, the United States is the only country in the world where foreigners from all parts of the world attempt to enter America. This seems to be for two main reasons – 1) the opportunity to raise their standard of living, and 2) to suppress oppression from their respective country of origin. This is often referred to as hope and opportunity.

No other country on the face of the globe offers the opportunity to grow and prosper without government intervention or the rule of law that opposes the potential for personal prosperity. I have personally made several friends over the years from Mexico and other counties, all of whom have managed to come into America and abide by our laws and they have prospered from not only a financial perspective, but also a familial perspective, becoming parents, grandparents and productive citizens. I for one can't fault a person from trying to improve through hard work or through education. These opportunities are possible in a capitalistic system not seen anywhere else in the world.

Presently, illegal immigration is costing American billions of dollars. The southern borders of the United States offer no barriers to immigrants to come into our country undictated, with hope of a better living for themselves and their immediate families. The general public does not have any problems with people entering our country for a better way of life. The problem is the enormous amount of individuals invading our borders with present numbers of over 100,000 per month. When entering America, our government is charged with the task of protecting people, offering shelter and food; not to mention medical care assistance needed for families whom have been living in the open for weeks and months at a time in trying to get to a country which offers hope, freedom and opportunity.

A barrier or wall is necessary to control the great influx of families to allow for an orderly process while protecting human rights. Over the past twenty-years there are editorials from both Democratic as well as Republicans saying a barrier is needed. This simple barrier will allow an orderly process to be established without the risk of lives for immigrants who want to enter America with their families for a better life.

Over the past 40-years, in Texas the counties along the Texas/Mexico border have experienced hundreds of thousands of new births associated with illegal immigrants who have crossed the border while pregnant. Present law offers any child of any mother born in America to be eligible for a social security number. The social security law needs to change, if parents are not already citizens of the United States, then no social security number will be issued to the new born. This act alone will stop the practice of pregnant women risking their lives and the lives of their unborn just for the sake of obtaining a social security number.

8. The Media

For several decades the late Walter Cronkite represented the main line media and the reporting thereof. Mr. Cronkite was viewed as the most respected and accurate reporter during his time. Mr. Cronkite reported the news as just that, news while never giving his opinion on any subject. Today's media ratings are based upon viewers and current media content pushes sensationalism as news of interest. News today is based upon controversy as being newsworthy. The kind act of a local Boy Scout assisting an older lady while crossing the street is not newsworthy. On the other hand, a scandal with a Senator and his mistress offers the general public gossip and is considered newsworthy. Maybe the media is right, as news is often a reflection of society.

The major networks have lead news anchors that are often household names, but each anchor now feels compelled to offer their personal opinion of any news situation. If one were to go back about 10-years, Dan Rather, probably the most recognized news anchor after Walter Cronkite, lost his job when taking a story to the public without exploring the authentication of the story, while taking a side of the story source. This one reporting incident led to Mr. Rather's early retirement. His career will be remembered for this one professional discretion based upon his choice of allowing his personal opinion to be made public. Dan Rather from Wharton, Texas made the national news scene with the landing of Hurricane Carla in the early 1960's in Brazoria and Galveston counties, Texas.

The media in today's world often shape public opinion. The viewer of the local daily news allows each viewer to keep abreast of the newsworthy events of the day. News anchors often report the news, but these same anchors allow their personal opinion to enter into their reporting. This personal opinion when added to the facts often distorts the facts of the report when the networks allow these editorials to be included by anchors. Therefore, the network often has an accompanying disclaimer associated with news anchor.

Another media personality whom has been employed by ABC, a co-anchor of Good *Morning* America, the host of ABC's Sunday morning *This Week* has been in the media forefront since his time as "communications director for the 1992 presidential campaign of Bill Clinton." (Wikipedia, 2019). The ABC network, as all networks, has an interest in increased ratings, and allowing George Stephanopoulos to report political issues in a biased manner is contrary to the Walter Cronkite era of journalism. Many in the general public have always placed their trust in news reports for accurate and timely reporting. This childlike acceptance has been defused with the likes of Stephanopoulos who wishes to insert his personal ideology into the daily broadcast. There is no place in media for journalism of this nature.

9. Foreign Trade - China

Over the past century, America has become the select consumer in the world. All countries, especially countries that have a weak currency and high exchange rate with the US Dollar, often target America for exporting goods manufactured with their respective country. The balance of trade between America and other countries in the world has historically placed the USA in a deficit position. For the year 2019, the news in the media was directed toward China with a lessor amount to Mexico.

No President of the United States has addressed the foreign trade debt and the imbalance thereof as seen with China. The inflows and outflows between these two countries are very disproportionate as the political arena has considered this area a "hot potato" and politically a no-win situation. Many an economist have declared this area of trade and commerce a very delicate process and as we can now see the opposing political party is in the media each and every day trying to convince the public of President Trump playing with fire. But the true historical assessment from Washington shows no President ever attempting to bring this trade deficit back into line with normal trade and commerce between countries.

Foreign trade represents the second of two issues the Trump administration is trying to bring under control. The first issue being illegal immigration and the second being foreign trade imbalance. China prior to their emergence as a manufacturing country has developed a long term strategy to mercantile the world, beginning with America. Beginning in the early 21st century, Mexico was the provider of much of our manufacturing while working within the auspices of NAFTA. NAFTA began with the Clinton Administration in 1994. China and their exchange rate coupled with their tremendous number of workers offered goods and services to be produced cheaper than that seen with Mexico.

With the beginning of years 2002-2004, there was a move abreast to move manufacturing into China due to their cheap labor which at the time was lower than Mexico. The Mexican Peso in 2000 had a US Dollar exchange rate of approximately 12-1. Presently the Peso to the dollar is about 19-1. China has the largest population in the world but lacks jobs for their ever-growing population in a State-owned enterprise.

With the Department of Homeland Security working with foreign Mexican officials, the threat of the Cartel has been greatly diminished over the last couple of years. The Cartels will never cease, as the opportunity to make large sums of quick money is always there. Coupled with the ease of illegal immigrants to enter the USA, the drug trade has prospered with the current USA appetite for illegal drugs. However, the level of Cartels growth has been somewhat limited due to both the USA and Mexico intervention. Thus the entrance of China as the global producer of goods and services.

USA manufacturers who outsourced their manufacturing of almost every type of product have experienced early savings, but over the time period of beginning in 2015, the wage advantage China had over Mexico began to disappear. Additionally, the manufacturing chain logistically was a three-month process with customary pay terms of half down upon the order and the balance due prior to export from mainland China. The smaller USA company would have to have adequate cash flow to weather the three-month negative flow for inventory. The logistical chain for Mexico with the assistance of NAFTA, could allow a Mexico manufacturer product to be order, produced and delivered back into the States within 30-days; thus, saving the USA company cash flow.

Why did China even enter the picture with the massive exodus from Mexico to China? This writer believes most USA companies did not want to subject their employees who traveled into Mexico with the up and coming Cartels associated with the drug lords. For several years starting in early 2004, there were weekly killings, murders of Mexican mayors and other elected officials. This one series of events allowed the swing of manufacturing power from Mexico to China.

"The US trade deficit with China was $336 billion in 2017, representing more than half the overall US trade deficit (Census, 2018). According to the 2018 US trade deficit, the balance grew to $621 billion according to the US Census (Amadeo, 2019). The US trade deficit with China from 1985 to present has gone from a trade balance of $3,855.7 of export to $3,861.7 or a healthy exchange of goods and services. But since 1985 the deficit has grown drastically to levels unseen in our global economy.

China, being a Communist Country, is a country that does not allow freedom of religion, and their birth control policy requires the medical community in China to kill babies while in the mother's womb. The cultural differences are immense. The leader of the Chinese is appointed for life, and this process leaves much room for graft and corruption. Our way of life is democracy and capitalism. The Chinese policy over the past 30-years has been to mercantile the world while at the same time manipulating their currency as well as moving large amounts of cash to support various commodity products, such as steel, etc.

With a cheaper Yuan, importers from China can buy more goods at a lower price in their specific currency. China is far removed from a capitalistic country, as the government often moves large sums of Yuan to support specific Chinese products. "The Chinese government has numerous State owned enterprises" (Hsu, 2018) and these state owned enterprises receive a larger share of loans than other types of enterprise (Hsu, 2018). "Although they employ only 16% of China's workers, they receive 30% of all the bank loans" (Hsu, 2018).

To complicate the trade difference, you also have the compounding problems of tariffs and currency manipulation. With the Chinese strategy to mercantile the world, full employment is brought about by China being the primary manufacturer for global consumption. With a Communist society, having low unemployment for the people is a good thing to have. China being large in nature has been in retrospective a third-world county, but over the past 35-years they have become a leading country in several areas. China being the largest populated country in the world with a large workforce live in a country "with a population of 1.3 billion people needing employment in order to raise their standard of living" (Amadeo, 2019). "China's leaders are afraid of revolt if growth isn't fast enough" (Amadeo, 2019). Chinese political leaders need to keep control of their general population for their own personal preservation of power and control. Not too different from the Congress here in the United States. Appease the public in general in order to continue our political lifestyle, hence the professional politician.

Trade tariffs are used to cover the budgets associated with personnel, facilities and equipment used to inspect goods imported into their respective country. An enormous task at best for any government, especially that of the United States which imports millions of goods and services daily. "Approximately 96% of US merchandise imports are industrial (non-agricultural) goods. The United States currently has a trade-weighted average import tariff rate of 2.0 % on industrial goods. One-half of all industrial goods entering the United States are duty free." (ustra.gov/industrial-tariffs, 2019).

The Chinese "have tariff rates 25% for a particular import, such as automobiles that are significantly higher than US tariff rates (2.5 percent) for imported automobiles (Chow & Sheldon, 2019). China has been using a large portion of their import tariffs to finance their government with their State owned companies. The excess tariffs are often used as loans to both the public sector as well as well as the private sector. "State owned enterprises in general receive a larger share of loans than other types of enterprises. Although they employee only 16% of China's workers, they receive 30% of all bank loans (Hsu, 2018).

10. Cultural Differences

Every country making up the sovereign 195 countries of the world have distinctive cultures as seen from other countries. One can further divide countries as to third-world or progressive countries as well as the super powers. These countries can be divided further into Democracy, Communist, Monarchy, Federal and a Dictatorship.

"The Communist form of government strongly emphasizes the central state, with very little private enterprise and almost everything owned by the government" (Sim, 2017). Both China and Russia are represented by the Communist Party. The Chinese are controlled by the National People's Congress whose members vote on the President of China.

During the George W. Bush tenure in the White House, "the incident is the Bush administration's first real foreign-policy crisis" (CNN, 2001). The results of this mid-air accident allowed the Chinese and their President Jiang Zemin to remove the US surveillance equipment to reverse engineer the technology developed by the US. Having reverse engineer the technology allowed the ability to "cut the US lead in electronic warfare by at least a decade (Beaver, 2001).

Moving forward to the 1990s, one Houston, Texas company involved in the seismic industry had a public offering and the offering allowed the company to form a software company located in China while employing several PhD Chinese programmers. Over the course of time, these programmers developed several successful programs for use in the seismic industry. While on an unannounced trip into China, the president of the company found his newly written software was being sold literally out of the back door to other seismic competitor companies. Thus, the company president shut down the new entity with great regret for even starting a China based company, although he had previously been advised regarding the culture of the Chinese and the probable outcome.

Moving forward another 10-years to the mid 1990's, another seismic processing company with which I was formerly involved had the exact same situation, where the fully employed Chinese programmers again were selling code literally out the back door. Another cause and effect relationship directed back to the Chinese culture.

"The United States is an example of a federal government, where the central federal government's powers are constrained by local and state authorities"(Sim, 2017). America represents opportunity and hope. The American standard of living when compared to the world's view of living conditions offers no one country to compare. This in part is why the United States is seeing their southern borders over run by over 100,000 illegal immigrants per month. One word can describe the reasons behind this phenomenon: opportunity.

Mexico can be considered a third-world country, as the general working population work under a collective bargaining system. The Mexico worker is diligent, pride full and family oriented. Mexico often reminds this writer of the 1950's era in America, as a time of family unit with religion playing a central role. The 50-years following the 1950s has seen a technology driven economy and the beginning of a drug culture as never before seen in this great nation. This drug culture has created what many view in America as a social choice to participate in the drug culture, but only to witness more powerful drugs, addiction and a life of misery for the individual as well as family members and friends whom often witness this human being's demise.

11. Employment in America

As of August 2019; America has the lowest pre or post war unemployment rates in the history of our country for both genders, all nationalities and for each culture represented. There are presently more jobs available then there are candidates for these positions.

With full employment, the American consumer can contribute to a large portion to our economy. Presently the economic conditions of our nation are prospering at levels not seen in recent decades. The demand for goods and services are allowing Americans to prosper as never seen before, primarily brought about by full employment. Not all Americans are wealthy but comparing the American standard of living to third-world countries, the outside immigrant sees capitalism as opportunity. No other country in the world has the same problems with immigration as the numbers of foreigners wanting to relocate to America is great. This is not seen with the other super powers such as China, Japan and Russia.

We live in a fast-paced world; the newly born infants in America will be faced with new jobs which haven't even been created as of today. It has been published that "65% of the future jobs have not been invented" (Davidson, 2017). Looking forward, education from a college and university perspective as well as technical schools will have to continue to grow while preparing our future workers.

12. National Debt

According to news releases, our national debt is over $22 trillion and climbing. Many an economist has come to the defense of the size of the debt saying this is only a percentage of our total Gross National Product (GNP). But from a practical purpose, out national government is financed by debt along with federal taxes imposed on both individuals and corporations.

When our government issues any debt instrument for any amount over any term, when the instrument becomes due and payable, the government has a history of adding the accrued interest to the debt and then rolling out the same debt with the added accrued interest. In breaking this debt process to the individual family unit, by the time a person would to retire, they would owe millions of dollar and they would not have the cash flow to service the debt instrument.

At this present writing, the Trump administration is in negotiations with the Chinese pertaining to our trade deficit which is historical between our two governments. This process will continue till the 2020 elections come into play, as the Chinese will never settle. The Chinese plan is to kick the can another year down the road in hopes of a Democratic victory in the White House. As previously mentioned, the Chinese do not operate in the same manner of a sovereign government, but that of a day-trader who will float huge amounts of money in order to make a short term profit. The Trump administration is countering with increased tariffs for any product from China entering into the United States. These tariffs mean billions of import dollars into the government coffers and the Trump administration might be well advised to take these funds and apply toward the national debt.

The late financial author Larry Burkett wrote a book entitled "The Coming Economic Earthquake", one of the earlier books predicting the future problems the United States would have in servicing debt. Larry points out with his research and statistical analysis there would be a point in time that the interest paid on the debt would be the largest line item in the federal budget. But, as seen today, the government does not pay the interest as they roll up the interest into the debt instrument and put out the new debt instrument for another 30-years; thus conversing cash flow, but increasing the federal deficit. Presently, "the national debt is over $22 trillion as of March 2019" (Xinhua News Agency, 2019).

13. America Today

There has been a move in America over the past decade of socialism as ushered in by the Democratic Party. "Socialism is a philosophy of failure, the creed of ignorance, and the gospel of envy, its inherent virtue is the equal sharing of misery", Winston Churchill (University of Phoenix, 2019). One only has to look at our Venezuelan neighbor and their present condition; socialism does not work for the masses, but it works only for a few in their society.

During the after WWII years, America was engulfed with the family unit, women back from the factories and men whom lived through the war-torn years; all were back to their safety of America. The family unit was growing, a person did not have to lock their homes and they could even leave their car keys in the ignition while in their local town during their weekly shopping.

Many of the small towns could see trucks with guns racks, now times have changed.

Neighbors and neighborhoods were places of visiting and kids playing outside in the yards or even in the street. In fact, in my small town of Lake Jackson, Texas, located south of Houston, Texas and 16-miles from the Texas Gulf Coast, had an abundance of mosquitos whereby the city would send out mosquitos spraying trucks which often filled the streets with a smoke like substance known as DDT. Little did we know, DDT was a major cancer-causing chemical used often, but during the 1950's kids would play in the smoke and often rode their bikes for several blocks in playing in the DDT.

Fast forward 70-years, technology engulfs each and every person on a daily basis. The printed newspaper is obsolete, computers are now in each of our hands and the front yards of the subdivision houses are vacant of kids outside playing. We now live in an information world, with information often confused with intelligence. The automobile industry is now in the process of converting from the combustion engine to the battery powered vehicle.

Medical and environmental advancements have progressed more in the past 40-years as compared to the history of man.

The world as we know it is much smaller due to communications and travel developments. Trade between countries located all over the world has allowed the supply chains to promote higher GNP for the third-world countries. Education offers opportunity and in America there is always the resources available to pay for one's education. Presently, for this generation, "65% of the future jobs in America haven't been invented" (Davidson, 2017). We now live in a fast-paced world.

America has been blessed and prosperity is available for all whom seek for a better quality of life. America offers opportunity; this is the one residing fact about America as compared to all of the countries in the world. Immigrants seek the opportunity to work and prosper in America. No other country has a rule of law that is consistent which protect property rights. There is not another country in the world that immigrants are eager to inhabit.

But America does have problems and many of these problems are seen in Washington DC whereby Congress votes on legislature by party lines and not about the law. The smart businessman is nowhere to be seen in DC, as the recipe for a politician is that of first being an attorney and secondly being a good orator.

America has a financial crisis waiting in the wings. Our national debt is out of control and this topic of having a balanced budget is not a politically correct topic. The American public knows of these issues, and their opinion of how to deal with DC can be seen in the results of the polls. President Donald Trump was elected to clear up DC. The establishment prior to the Trump administration, fought tooth and nail to prevent a new party in DC, and much to everyone's amazement, a non-politician was ushered in office.

During my career, my work included doing financial workouts for troubled companies. The Trump administration is in the same, albeit much more complex, position that involves hundreds of millions of Americans as well as other countries around the world that rely on the strength and support of the United States of America. Donald Trump is one of a few men qualified to change Washington DC. Somewhat of a turnaround specialist, Trump has the vision and the stomach to handle the task, a task that is immense in size. Resistance is fierce and we as the public have seen firsthand how the opposing party will use any method available to maintain their positions of power, money and greed.

As Americans, we should all respect the office of the President of the United States. This position is the most powerful office in the world. We should support the President in his strategy to bring back America to greatness and watch history being made. No other President in our history has had such a large task at hand. The silent majority has spoken. For the opposing party, you will have the opportunity to vote your personal convection during the upcoming 2020 elections.

14. Education

Many a new residing party in both the houses of Congress often relate to educational reform. The same can be said by the newly elected Governors of each state, as one of their main election promises revolves around education. Education is always a bandwagon issue which all Americans will accept as a much needed area.

The educational rally has been much ado about nothing. If one were to study education changes, there has never been any talk of working with students who are not college material, but these students will work somewhere within our society. Neither is there a program designed to mentor, educate or direct students during their high school years. There could be a preparation process whereby each high school in the United States could offer career counselors in a regulated program beginning the freshman year of high school.

The program would begin with each school district or parish having from 1-5 career counselors on staff with a mission statement of educating each student as to identifying what the student passion is, what educational opportunities are out in the world and to develop a plan to meet their personalized individual goal. The program could be broken down into three major areas:

1. Identifying what the student wants to become, or where their passion lies.
2. Development of a personalized plan to achieve their passion.
3. Plan implantation.

Each major area of the plan can further be broken down into college or trade school, testing required, and a road map to how to achieve where the student wants to go. Preparation is critical for students at such a young age.

In Texas we have a counselor whom could develop such a program: a PhD named Dr. Roxie Halekakis Gilchrist, an educational counselor for the Magnolia Independent School District while working at Magnolia High School. Dr. Halekakis Gilchrist would be the perfect educator to initiate this program in Texas as her heart is for the student.

Presently in Texas the education system is designed to teach students as to pass the STAAR test. The State of Texas Assessments of Academic Readiness (STAAR tests) are standardized tests taken by most Texas public school students in the spring of each year during grades 3-12" (Hochberg, 2018). Standardized testing is important to monitor and compare historical testing results. But, there is no plan in place for the student who has no desire to continue with a college education. An alternative system needs to be in place to allow students to understand their strengths and weaknesses as well as their preference regarding a career in today's world. Similar to a SWOT Analysis (Strengths, Weakness, Opportunity, Threat) A specific career counseling program might be the solution for a large majority of students.

15. Where do we go from Here?

The world today has been made closer than ever when viewing travel and communications. Capitalism has offered cross-country business relationships to all parts of the world. America has become the consumer of global products produced whereby each country hopes to manufacture goods for consumers in America. The Communist countries seek to keep their people gainfully employed at the numerous state-owned companies thereby creating an economy of full employment with expectations of higher standard of livings for their peoples.

The super-powers are the global leaders which all countries often follow and typically attempt to adopt their rule of law in working with the other governments of the world. The NAPTA agreement is one of these accords form in 1994 under the Clinton administration which allows for the movement of goods and services between Canada, the United States and Mexico.

As Americans, we are not going to change the culture of the other 194 countries in the world, but we can offer opportunity to work with each in some form. These forms can be seen with normal currency exchange rates, foreign trade or even allowing America to be their police force.

Immigration is another important factor when viewing the field of education. Many a global leader has come to America during their college years to be educated by the various American colleges and universities. Often these foreign students go back to their respective countries in positions of influence and having seen firsthand how America works. Hong Kong is now going through growing pains of wanting to move away from the Communistic way of life to that of opportunity. Only time will allow for these walls to eventually fall, but at what cost?

The American two party systems have failed, and as a reminder our first President of the United States in his farewell message to Congress had these words of wisdom continuing for over 224-years. First, George Washington warned of "the baneful effects of the Spirit of the Party" (UShisotry.org,

2019). "To Washington political parties were a deep threat to the health of the nation for they allowed a small but artful enterprising minority to put in the place of the delegated will of the Nation, the will of the party." (UShisotry. org, 2019).

President Washington was in effect saying the wants and needs of the party often overrule the delegate and his constituents that elected him to represent their views and desires while being in office as their delegate. Washington was very profound in his findings and these findings are very much seen with our two-party political system.

How can we change this process in America? Our political culture has been embedded in or Democracy for hundreds of years; change could happen, but again, at what cost? In this writer's opinion, the current two-party systems do not allow the new elected official to rise to the top. In all levels of society there is always a person that has views and opinions where many of the general population view as healthy. This person can be considered an up and coming leader who could alter public opinion; but with the two-party systems, any aspiring recognized leader is often held back to the current reigning political party leaders.

We the people need to study and elect the delegates whose views that mostly reflect our personal convictions. The fight and support for such a delegate will be tedious at best, but this process is the only way to bring forth candidates whose ideology reflects that of the general populous. This could happen, as evidenced by the results of the 2008 and the 2016 Presidential elections, each nominee was reflective of what the general populous wanted, that of change in Washington DC. The 2016 election proved the resolve of the silent majority in electing a non-political person to the highest office of the land. But why did this phenomenon happen?

The American peoples want change. The results of the 2016 election showed the world the American people are not happy with high taxation, they wanted a voice in government, the general opinion of DC from the general population is reflective of a government that is totally out of control and the financial state of our nation is on the verge of default due to increasing national debt that no political leader wishes to discuss. A spiraling economy headed toward a brick wall.

America was founded by our forefathers as a Christian nation under God. With our humble beginning, we as a country have moved far away from our founding fathers vision. As Americans need to go back to basics, the Bible offers solutions to many of our national problems, but first we need to acknowledge a higher being, that with the Lord Jesus Christ. Once this acknowledgement is made by each of us, the healing process can begin. Let us not waste time with the political process in arguing each of our positions, but move forward as scripture directs each of us to live in an orderly and responsible manner.

References

1. Xinhua News Agency 2019.
2. Hutson, Barry F. (2019*) Congressional Research Service: Report 5/8/2019*, preceding p1-18, 21p.
3. Adler, Lee (2017). *The Social Security Trust Fund is Just a Stack of IOUs in a West Virginia Filing Cabinet.* The Wall Street Examiner.
4. Sim, Philip (2017). *5 Types of Government & Their Characteristics.* Classroom, 2001-2009, Leaf Group Ltd.
5. ustra.gov/industrial-tariffs, 2019.
6. Chow, Daniel C.K. & Sheldon, Ian 2019. *Is Strick Reciprocity Required for Fair Trade?*
7. CNN 2001. *US Spy Plane Crashes in China: Chinese Strip Plane of Sensitive Equipment.*
8. Beaver, Paul 2001. *China Returns Crew of Downed US Spy Plane, Keeps Plane.*
9. Wikipedia 2019. *Stephanopoulos. George*
10. Davidson, Cathy 2017. *65% of Future Jobs Haven't Been Invented Yet?*
11. Hochberg, Scott, 2019.